Recollections

An Artist and Writer Recalls Ten Unusual and Totally Unique Events in His Life

Harry C. Doolittle

iUniverse, Inc.
Bloomington

Recollections
An Artist and Writer Recalls Ten Unusual and
Totally Unique Events in His Life

iUniverse books may be ordered through booksellers or by contacting:

iUniverse
1663 Liberty Drive
Bloomington, IN 47403
www.iuniverse.com
1-800-Authors (1-800-288-4677)

Because of the dynamic nature of the Internet, any web addresses or links contained in this book may have changed since publication and may no longer be valid. The views expressed in this work are solely those of the author and do not necessarily reflect the views of the publisher, and the publisher hereby disclaims any responsibility for them.

Any people depicted in stock imagery provided by Thinkstock are models, and such images are being used for illustrative purposes only.

Certain stock imagery © Thinkstock.

ISBN: 978-1-4759-7204-7 (sc)
ISBN: 978-1-4759-7203-0 (e)

Library of Congress Control Number: 2013902861

Printed in the United States of America

iUniverse rev. date: 02/13/2013

Contents

Author's Preface

I should have entitled this book, *Remembrance of Things Past*, but alas, a much greater writer than I beat me to it. His name was Marcel Proust. And so, *Recollections* will have to do. And now to begin as my memory allows it...

Recruitment

Recollection #1:

Fall of 1943, World War II was at full swing, and I was twenty-years old. For the past two years I had been a U.S. Marine Corp reservist while at the same time attending Northwestern University in Evanston, Illinois. At that time, a call to active duty did not mean that I nor my fellow reservists, would have to fight. Instead, we were to be awarded the title, Private First Class, along with a marine corps uniform, and sent to reside at a "marine barracks." In my case, "barracks" meant an N.U. fraternity house.

The plan was to no longer have any of us remain as just a marine "grunt" (marine slang for privates and non-coms). Instead, the plan was for us, as college students, to become marine officers. This meant we marines were supposed to stay in college until we were needed, and then, when called, go to the officer's training school at Quantico, Virginia. There we were to be graduated as second lieutenants. How long was it before I would have to go? I figured a year; meanwhile as the war was raging worldwide the other marine reservists and I were supposed to remain in school. The reason for the delay, according to "scuttle-butt" (rumors) was that the marines already had a surfeit of officers and didn't need any more.

And so one day the time came when two dozen or so of my newly recruited fellow marines and I lined up in civilian clothes outside our "barracks:" in this case a fraternity house at the university. This was in early September 1943. We stood there, shoulder pressed against shoulder, wearing mostly T-shirts and jeans (our marine uniforms were due to arrive days later). And on the ground next to each marine was his suitcase containing his other clothes and personal effects.

Standing in front of this lineup were two men in uniform. The one in the background was a marine captain, and the other, in front of him and nearest to us, was a platoon sergeant. He was in charge with the captain being there as an observer only. His cap set at exactly the correct angle and his brown tie tucked inside his khaki shirt between the second and third button as marine regulations required. His shirt sleeves and blue pants had a red strip down each side (worn only by noncoms and officers), had been ironed razor sharp and the shine on his shoes blinded the eye.

So now the sergeant, let's call him Sergeant Lee, standing in front of us with his hands on his hips, barks out orders, "Attention! Line up! Tallest, left! Shortest, right! The rest stand in between!" After a lot of shuffling the line gets formed; tallest left, shortest right and the rest in between. Me? At six feet, I ended up amongst the few to the left. Sergeant Lee, again with hands on hips, shouts, "Attention! No talking!" I did my best to obey. Head up, shoulders back, stomach sucked in. As for talking, neither I nor anyone near me spoke a word, except for one person.

This was a guy standing three marines to my left. He was about my height and I did not know him, and in fact I had never seen him before. What set him apart from the rest of us and had raised the ire of Sergeant Lee was that he was talking, and mostly to himself. And not only that, his head was bobbing up and down, and he was laughing, giving the impression that he thought this whole procedure, as well as the sergeant, was a big joke.

Seeing this, Sergeant Lee walked over to him. He stopped and said, "Okay, Loudmouth, knock it off." But Loudmouth paid no attention and kept on chuckling. This was too much for the good sergeant. Standing back a few feet from his target, the sergeant made a tight right-hand fist. Then, with all his might, punched the marine in the stomach. It took but an instant, and Loudmouth began to gag and double over. Fortunately two marines on each side of him seeing this, grabbed him just before his head hit the ground. Still holding him, they backed out of the line, laid him down, and then returned to their places. Sergeant Lee, as cool and collected as if the incident had never occurred, stepped back while turning to face us, commanded: "Attention! Line up!" Then, "Dress right." Lastly, "Troops, dismissed!" And that was it. From then on, the only time we college marines saw the sergeant again was on the school's soccer field where he helped teach us how to march correctly. As for Loudmouth, no one saw him again.

So that was my introduction to the marines, as well as to the war. It was also the day I felt I was beginning to graduate from my own fantasy world and enter the real world of reality. Now, a question is: could an incident as described above be repeated by the marines of today? I doubt it. It just wouldn't happen. But things were different then. It was the early 1940's and almost every one of my twenty-year old frat brothers had left or was leaving school. All in which were headed into either the marines, army, navy, or the army air corps (later renamed air force). Therefore, there was scarcely an American family who did not have a sad war story to tell such as what happened to my Florida Uncle William's, and his wife Ruth's son, Bill.

In the spring of '43, their twenty-six-year old and only child, Bill, was piloting a four engine B-24 Flying Fortress ("B" being the Boeing Co., the plane's maker) on a bombing mission over Germany when a German pilot flying a single engine Messerschmitt 109 spotted his plane. This was followed by machine gun fire from the 109 which set all four of Bill's plane's engines ablaze and Bill had no choice except to don a parachute and bail out; all this having taken place at an altitude of 25,000 feet. Next, as the official report later stated, at 15,000 feet, the German pilot seeing Bill hanging beneath his parachute and continuing to float down, spun his M-109 around and machine gunned him. My cousin Bill was dead before he hit the ground.

Suddenly, this then leads my mind to the story of my eleven-month-older twenty-five-year old brother, Burling. He, like our cousin Bill, was a wartime pilot. And he, along with his co-pilot, flew a two-engine, cigar- shaped B-26 Marauder fighter/bomber. The word was that it was an extremely dangerous plane to fly and several were reported to have crashed with their young pilot trainees still aboard. One reason allegedly being that its wings were too narrow and short. At any rate, my brother had to fly the thing, and did so for twenty-five successful missions, taking off from a London U.S. Air Corps based airport to bomb Italian and German military airfields that lay across the channel. Leading to late 1943, with the required twenty-five missions under his belt, he came home, still remaining in the Air Corps.

But that's not the whole point of this story. The point is that, in the same room aboard the ship which took my brother to Europe, and war, in spring of 1943, were eleven other pilots, several of them B-26'ers. Of the twelve, only he and two others, neither a B-26'er, came home. Now was this because of the superiority of the enemy's flying capabilities or to an inferiority of the B-26 planes? No one will ever know. But one thing I do know, Jimmy Doolittle, the famed racing car driver, racing plane flyer and a war time four star Air Corps General, hearing about the B-26 controversy, asked that he be given a B-26 for his own official use. It's been reported that he thought it flew just great. But isn't that what you'd expect to hear from a Doolittle?

So now, everything you've read so far includes not only the beginning but the end of my marine corps career. It actually ceased in the spring of 1944 when I switched to the navy.

Reason? Word had reached me that while there was no longer a need for marine officers, there was a great need for navy ones, these to help in the execution and success of planned future landings of American troops on Japanese shores.

Which now brings me back to leaving Northwestern University. I soon found myself at Cornell College, located in Ithaca, New York, taking special Naval courses which would help prepare me to become a Navy Ensign. A quick three months later, along with my new uniform and an Ensign's gold bars, I arrived at Melville, Rhode Island. There, I was to be taught how to command a Navy PT (Patrol Torpedo) boat, which meant learning how to fight a different way of war than as a marine. My boat, PT 108, and I, saw duty in New Guinea, the Philippines, and Borneo; more of which I tell about in another chapter.

As an aside: during the war, and long before he became a U.S. President, John "Jack" Kennedy was also a PT CO (commanding officer). His boat was number 109, and its sinking by a Japanese destroyer and his return to the states, was and is legendary. But unfortunately, I never had the pleasure of meeting him, because before I went overseas he had gone home.

Written On Condition
of Anonymity

Recollection #2:

(Many VIP's in business, the military, and the government desire to get their thoughts out to the public while at the same time are reluctant to be named; like the CEO of a big U.S. company who, upon being questioned by the NY Times, said, "Please don't use my name" because he didn't want his board to know he was being interviewed. As did an Army General I spoke to who asked "not to be identified " ...and the White House official whom I called asking for an interview with him when I was working at the Chicago City News Bureau, and he said he'd speak "only on a condition of anonymity" because of the "delicate nature of the topic;" (and so, some of what follows is apocryphal, but a lot is not).

Dear Mr. Inquiring Reporter:

Rumor has reached me that your editor has assigned you to do a story about a VIP journalist like myself and I wish I could help, but I don't think I can.

According to my attorney (whose name I can't reveal because he practices on a condition of anonymity), I'm prohibited from writing to you and disclosing my true identity, which includes my name, gender, age, address, phone number and marital status.

However, my attorney has acknowledged that it's okay to write you that I'm around thirty-four years old, between five to six feet in height, weigh less than-but no more than-two hundred pounds and have hazel-green eyes. What's more, as a sop to me, he says it's all right to say I'm also a painter of abstract collages. But I'm not allowed to describe on paper the unique process I use to create such fantastically beautiful artwork, which if you saw it in person would immediately help you identify who I am.

This can be easily arranged by leaving your residence for a visit to NYC's Chelsea area. Here, 318 galleries are home to the works of hundreds of artists, including me. And because my lawyer won't let a VIP artist/writer like me tell you my name, nevertheless by your touring all of the 318 galleries you should be able to come upon it with almost no effort.

As you go from gallery to gallery, just pick out the paintings which you think look like abstract collages and then measure their frames with a tape measure. Those which turn out to be around 43" x 32" could be some of mine. But to be really sure, examine the writing at the bottom right hand corner on each painting that you think looks most like a collage. If you see a signature scribbled on the canvas with black ink and in clumsy block letters, that's my name.

But enough of that. Since my attorney won't let me identify myself when I write to you, or anyone else for that matter, the result is, I'm in VIP identity limbo. And right now this is an embarrassing place in which to be. For instance, today I promised my live-in partner I would write to Great Aunt Susie at 118 Pine St. East Moline, Illinois, to congratulate her on turning ninety-five.

Now I know what you're thinking... you'll get hold of that town's phone directory and search it until you find the name of the person who lives at that address and in that way you'll find out *my* name.

Sorry. Great Aunt Susie is my live-in partner's second cousin, once removed, and thus, as no kin of mine, she doesn't know me from Adam or Eve. Of course, you could use the phone and call her and ask: "Did you get a birthday card from out of town?" And she, who even at ninety-five still has all her marbles, would reply: "I sure did. It was from some nut who signed it anonymous."

Then, just suppose I wanted to get an art critic to review my latest painting. One way would be to mail a letter to the *Times* and ask the art editor to send a critic to my studio. Well, no one could blame the editor for thinking that he or she is dealing with a weirdo and not allow a reporter to visit me. Especially after not seeing a signature at the end of my letter, but instead "written on condition of anonymity."

That's not good. Think of how the editor might react if instead of writing to him or her I used the phone? After my speaking, "Hi there" the next thing my lawyer would require me to say is, "I'm speaking to you on a condition of anonymity, and. . . hello?. . .hello?"

No, that way is no good either. This brings me around to repeating. I'm not the right sort of VIP for you to interview. Even though I'm a great artist/writer and also have lived an incredibly exciting life, the straps on this straitjacket of un-identity in which I've been encased are being pulled tighter and tighter, thus preventing me from writing to you about things which have happened to me, to which could result in your authoring what could be a prize-winning article. Sorry about that.

So instead of interviewing a VIP like me, may I suggest a movie star? I've gotten to know several and can give you the names of some really famous ones whom I'm sure won't turn you down. Write him, or her, and mention my name, and . . . oops, I almost forgot. You'd be starting the letter with, "I'm writing you at the suggestion of a person who has written me on a condition of anonymity, and . . ." Well, what do you know? We're right back to where we started.

Yours truly, Anonymous.

Sharks Galore

America's war with Japan ended on August 5, 1945, resulting in many of America's military stationed in the Philippines to pack up and start to sail off to the good old U.S. of A. But alas, not me. I, still a Navy Lieutenant JG, remained at the country's southern Pacific Ocean seaside city, Samar, where PT Boat Squadron 10 was now based. My boat, PT 108, on which I had served as its CO (Commanding Officer) had been hauled onto dry land, laid on its side, and stripped of all of its armament; this consisted of its two torpedoes and all of its guns. Then, along with two other weapons- denuded PT hulks, were lifted by a crane, piled in a heap, and set on fire.

Destroying them this way, rather than having them returned to the U.S. via cargo ship, still useful to our navy, was the brain child of a McCarthy-like U.S. senator who harangued about not allowing the Russian navy to get hold of them, because the Russians might employ them against us. What nonsense!

Well, the burned PT boats fire's embers soon died down, and I began to wonder: what next? The answer came a few weeks later when I received orders to leave the Philippines and to report to a navy base at Guam. And I did, arriving there after a six-hour flight on a four-engine C-54 cargo plane, lying amongst its trunks and canvas bags. Stepping off the plane I turned around to thank the plane's pilot, who was close by, and my goodness, he was a kid, probably no more than eighteen but wearing Air Corps wings. Such a thing would be unthinkable today, having an eighteen-year-old boy piloting a giant four-engine plane, but that was all perfectly normal back in those days.

Still following orders, I hopped aboard a cab and reported to my final destination; a 130 foot long all wooden U.S. Navy minesweeper, YMS 463. After saluting its flag and its captain, I went below to my tiny cabin with its two bunks, one on top of the other, and stowed my gear. It turned out I was just one of its five officers, only two of us really needed, but rather than have a lot of guys like us go home to jobs that didn't exist, it was thought by Washington politicals that it would be best to "keep the boys overseas" until the job situation improved. Great, except when you have three Navy officers having to live in a tiny cabin with just two bunks, that's another matter. But we survived.

Soon our orders came through stating that YMS 463 should proceed to the Truk Island atoll and lagoon, where a dozen or more Japanese World War II navy vessels, including destroyers and cruisers, lay rusting away in ocean water two hundred feet deep. Not only that, but also floating underneath its surface and close to the wrecks were 1,400 mines. Each was dropped there by Allied planes several years earlier in order to keep the Japanese warships from sailing from Truk intent on sinking any Allied shipping which might be passing by on its way to the Philippines.

Since our little YNS 465 was wooden, it was believed that all we had to do was to steam into Truk's mine-infested waters and do our thing: namely, dispose of the mines. This consisted of towing a long steel cable on which was attached to a device that would cut the wires attached to the mines, thereby making them rise to the water's surface. There, after being spotted by a sharpshooter standing on the YMS's stern with a rifle, each mine would be blown up with a single bullet. Sounds simple, but I wanted no part of it, and wished I was elsewhere.

Fortunately my wish was granted. It seems just prior to the time we were to proceed with this delightful task, one of our YMS's two diesel engines went kerplunk, and our ship's captain said, in effect, "We ain't sailing into any 1,400-mine field with just one engine!" So he gave orders to turn the ship around and we headed back for Guam.

But it wasn't long after, with both diesel engines now working, and our ship in mid-ocean, that our captain decided that since we hadn't done any real minesweeping, it might be a good idea to practice some. So he gave orders to stop the YMS and to deploy the mine sweeping cable. Once that was done, he gave orders to proceed. But it didn't happen. Disaster struck. The helmsman at the ship's controls, instead of pushing the forward lever, pushed the one for reverse. Result: we went backwards, which resulted in the cable towline getting caught in the ship's propellers. All engines were then stopped, leaving the ship silent and bobbing in the waves. Well, something had to be done, and I was the answer. It seems, since I was the only one on board with a scuba diver's license, I was appointed to go over the ship's side and see what was wrong. And I did, wearing a mask and my fins. It was hopeless. The rope was ensnarled beyond release. But I stayed and continued to tread water. That's when I noticed it; a shark about ten feet long circling around and around behind me. As it did, its head swiveled to and fro as if trying to decide if I was edible or not. Strangely, no one on the ship's deck above me seemed to notice it, which was not reassuring. So as fast as I could, I scrambled up the ship's ladder and back on deck, leaving the shark still circling.

The captain, after hearing my report about the entangled rope, snapped his fingers, and a seaman arrived with an axe. In one swing the rope was cut and we watched it, along with an attached buoy, big knife, and flag, slowly drift away. And what happened to the rope and its companions? Like the 1,400 underwater ocean mines, they may all still be at sea.

It was now December 1945, and the YMS, with me still aboard, was ordered to proceed to the Bikini Islands to take part in America's first over-the-ocean atomic bomb test. Two similar bombs had previously been dropped in early August on the Japanese cities, Hiroshima and Nagasaki, partially destroying them along with hundreds of thousands of their citizens and thus bringing the war to an end on August 5th. Now the plan was to learn what such a bomb could do to a group of enemy naval vessels. And so to find out, our Navy had collected a huge group of no-longer-useful battleships, destroyers, cruisers, and merchants, and had them anchored inside the Bikini atoll.

The plan was to then put an atomic bomb on board an unmanned B-24 Flying Fortress, using radio signals from the ground to fly it and at 30,000 feet have it drop the bomb onto the anchored and assembled ships. This was to be followed by having other ships stationed outside the atoll, including our YMS, return to the atomic bombed water. Once there, using Geiger counters, have ichthyologists (marine life scientists) measure the amount of radiation emanating from the tons of irradiated metal, the millions of gallons of irradiated ocean water, and the thousands of irradiated fish left there after the bombing. The measurements were scheduled to take place both before and after the bombing. The first to learn how radioactive the water was, and the second to learn how much the radiation had increased, if at all. And how was this to be done? Well, instead of measuring the ocean's water for irradiation, the plan was to measure its sea life, primarily fish. So that's what our YMS and its crew were called on to help do.

We were to "tag" fish, mostly sharks, none less than five feet long. And after lifting one out of the water, we were to staple an aluminum tag onto a fin which gave the date when and place where it been captured. Just how was the ship's crew and its ichthyologists supposed to do this? The first step was to entice the sharks to come along the ship's side and once there to have a crew member lean over (a mere five feet above the water) and, after inserting a boat hook into its gills, flip the shark onto the deck, leaving its tail frantically flap, flap, flapping, still very much alive.

Next, one of the onboard ichthyologists would approach it and, using a small air gun, insert a tiny metal disk into one of its fins marking the date and place where all this was taking place. The idea was that after all the tagged sharks were thrown back into the ocean, as many of the tagged sharks as possible would be picked up again, thus allowing the scientists to determine how many of the estimated sharks that had been in the lagoon in the first place had survived. Thus they would get an idea of how effective the atomic bombing had been.

But how did the crew get the sharks to swim so close to the YMS? They did so by inviting them to dinner. Huge quantities of offal (the insides of a sheep's carcass) had been brought along for just this purpose. Tossed into the ocean, it performed like catnip for cats. Within minutes the YMS's hull was surrounded by dozens of offal-eating, teeth-gnashing, wiggling sharks, none shorter than six feet. It seemed there were so many one could walk on them. And so the hauling out and tagging went on, and on, with snapping sharks now lying on deck waiting to be tagged. So many, that one could hardly see the deck's surface beneath them. Me? I took a last look and headed back to my cabin.

What happened next? I was due to return home, and just in time, as the YMS was scheduled to return the following week to the about-to-be-atomic- bombed ship cemetery. Luckily, there was an American LST about to leave Bikini, and so getting my luggage together, I hopped aboard as a passenger. Stopping in Hawaii, I then hitched a ride on a C-47's baggage section, which later touched down at an army air corps air field near San Francisco. From there I bummed a ride, lying on parachutes inside the freezing-cold belly of a single-engine navy torpedo plane, where the torpedo was usually kept, eventually landing at a small airport west of Chicago. Lastly, hitching a ride to Evanston, Illinois, where my home was.

Now why did it take such a circuitous and crazy way for me to get there? Who knows? Maybe it was because so many of the Washington's political biggies couldn't care less about the thousands of America's militaries who were still overseas. While I didn't mind, I was disappointed that I hadn't done what

I later learned a couple of army air corps officers had done after leaving Bikini.

The story being they hopped aboard an Air Corps cargo transport going to Hong Kong then to Leningrad to see its art museum, to Cairo to see its pyramids and to Paris to see the French Folies-Bergère. Stopping lastly at London to tour the Queen Palace: all before finally returning home and there to be discharged. During that entire trip (I believe it took a year), they continued to wear their uniforms and to receive Army Air Corps pay. And it didn't cost them a cent because everywhere they went grateful citizens greeted them as heroes and picked up all tabs, including meals at the finest restaurants and stays at the most expensive hotels. Ah, could I have only been so clever! Still, it felt great just to arrive home at the U.S. of A.

Chicago's City News Bureau

Recollection #4:

I was just one of several of young persons wanting to learn how to become a newspaper reporter who was lucky enough to get a job at the City News Bureau of Chicago in 1948. Our assignments were to include covering every single death recorded in the coroner's office, every important meeting, and just about any other incident that occurred in the city, day or night. The information we gathered was then to be passed on, almost always by telephone, to editors at the city's major newspapers.

These were the *Chicago Tribune*, the *Sun Times*, and the *Daily News*. And some of its graduates who had preceded me and went on to fame and fortune after leaving the CNP were the playwright Charles MacArthur, the *New York Times* columnist David Brooks, the pop artist, Claes Oldenburg, and the novelist, Kurt Vonnegut. Quite an illustrious group.

I worked eight hours a day and often the same amount of time at night, starting in the evening five days a week. I arrived there from my home in Evanston, a northern Chicago suburb, commuting to and fro by train. The term "police reporter" most accurately describes my job. What this meant was being sent from CNB's downtown headquarters to hang out at the city precinct's police stations; some days going to one and then on to several others on Chicago's West Side. Some days going to a few on its north side, and some days to a few on its South Side. That way I got to know Chicago's streets and buildings, about as well as anyone ever had. My means of travel was the street car (in almost any other city except Chicago it would be called a trolley). Fares were ten cents a ride, and I was given a fistful of dimes to carry in my pocket by a nice lady at the CNB headquarters when I reported in each day before heading out.

I then began a routine which I followed at the beginning of every work day. This consisted of leaving CNB's offices and walking west on Madison Street across the Chicago River Bridge to arrive at my first police station stop of the day. It was located in what could only be called a "skid row," consisting of a red brick building with a large steel-barred cell in its basement. And locked inside were dozens of poor souls, always men, who had been picked up from Chicago's West Madison Street's sidewalks, totally intoxicated and barely able to walk or talk. How had they come to be there and in such a state? Almost all had arrived by train, crammed inside freight box cars, via one or another of the five U.S. railroads which came to Chicago from every part of the country. They had come looking for work (remember the Depression was still on, especially in the West and South). Being that meals were not part of freight train service meant each had to carry his own eatables, along with something to drink, which for many meant booze. This, plus for what they also could buy for very little money at a liquor store, along with their loneliness, and joblessness was the catalyst that led to such widespread inebriation.

And so, I entered the West Madison Street police station (that's *street* and not *avenue* as in New York) and presented myself to the desk sergeant, showing him my press card. That's when it hit me. The most god-awful stench I had ever smelled. Where was it coming from? From the police station's basement, where there was an enormous cell in which all the police station's prisoners were incarcerated. It was a horror! No showers, a toilet that barely flushed and a cold-water faucet that dripped. The floor was concrete, and those prisoners which couldn't be accommodated by its few bunks slept on it amidst upchuck and urine. Two prisoners were assigned to mop up daily but it was to no avail. Me? I couldn't stand the stench, but the desk sergeant and his cohorts didn't seem to mind, apparently inured to it. I'm sure no such conditions as those exist there today.

And so after my obligated one-day stay, I hopped aboard a street car and went on to another police station, this one at Chicago's way out far West Side. Then, as I did at every station I was sent to, I would phone the main office to get an assignment. A typical one given me by one of CNB's editors would go like this: "There's been a shooting at [such and such a home]. Call' em at [he gives me the phone number] and get back to me."

And so I'd call and say, "Hello, I'm a reporter from the City News Bureau and I understand that someone in your home has been shot." And the voice at the other end would interrupt, screaming at me, saying something like, "How dare you call at a time like this!" And slam down the phone.

And so I'd call my editor back and say: "Hey, they don't want to talk and what'll I do?" And he'd say, "Listen kid, call' em back and get the g-d story!" And I did, only this time I'd say, "Hi, I'm a reporter working at the *Chicago Tribune*, and I understand there's been a shooting in your home."

Then I'd hear the voice at the other end, usually a woman's, shouting to her husband, saying, "Hey, Charlie, there's a *Tribune* guy on the phone, and he's asking about the shooting. And he says we're going to get our names in the paper!" And then, coming back to me on the phone, she says: "Okay, whaddaya-wanna know?" And I'd get the story.

Well, this sort of thing went on for a long time: my being assigned to get news about police arrests and auto accidents and then phoning the info about same to CNB's editors. And among them was an event more unusual than any of the others, about which I'm going to tell you now.

It began with a phone call from my office to me when I was at one of Chicago's West Side police stations, Orders were for me to get myself out to the county morgue, a part of the Cook

County Hospital, which was located just over the city's border. And there I was to look at the dead body of one of Chicago's more notorious gangsters (whose name I was never told) and to report the number of bullet holes on his dead body, the bullets of course being the cause of his demise. And so I arrived, and the morgue's supervisor rolled out a concrete slab on which his naked body was lying. Sure enough there were three bullet holes, now looking like little round red blotches on his skin: two in his stomach area, and one right over the heart.

I then glanced down, my eyes focusing on his feet, and lo and behold, each of his toenails had been painted a bright red. What's this, I ask myself? Could this rough-tough fifty-year-old gangster also have been gay? I then looked closely at his dead face, and on it was a small grey mustache, and a little pointed gray beard, along with grey sideburns, and black hair: not the face of a gay guy, I tell myself. But if not, then why the red toenails? And then it hits me.

No matter what kind of person he was, there must have been a wife who adored him, or perhaps it was his seven-year-old granddaughter who felt the same way. And either could have painted his toenails. The little girl first sitting on his lap, and saying, "Grandpa, can I paint your toenails?"

And laughing, he says "Sure." Or maybe it was his wife: "Honey, your brother and his wife are coming over for dinner this evening. Let's have some fun, and let me paint your toenails. It'll make them laugh." And he, also laughing, replies, "Sure."

Well, no one will ever know if it really happened like that, but if it did, it's something to ponder.

Charlton Heston

Recollections #5:

"*Et tu*, Brutus!" These words are from Shakespeare's play, *Julius Caesar*. But this time they were not being spoken by a renowned New York Broadway actor, but instead by a teenage Charlton Heston in a 16mm black- and-white film in which he was making his debut as a movie actor, was produced and shot by another film enthusiast and teenager, David Bradley, who lived in the same town as I did, Winnetka, Illinois, a suburb twelve miles north of Chicago. And this was just one of several amateur movies which I believe David made using Charlton in the leading role of each one. Others included *Macbeth*, *King Lear*, and Ibsen's *Peer Gynt*.*

At that time, it was the mid 1930's, Charlton and I were both attendees at Winnetka's New Trier High school, and he and I being of the same age were in the same grades. I lived in Winnetka, and he in nearby Willamette, both villages being part of a large township. While this was in the middle of the Depression, when it came to spending money there was no holding back on the amounts the township's taxpayers where willing to contribute toward the education of its high school students.

Result: New Trier offered classes the likes of which I doubt whether any other high school in the country at that time did.

These included a complete machine shop where boys could bring in a twenty-five-dollar wreck of a car and learn how to repair it; a part-time golf pro who taught the teenagers how to play the game; instructors in swimming and diving; musicians who helped organized teenage jazz bands; and best of all, teachers whose sidelines where teaching acting along with anything else having to do with theater. And for Charlton, this was like offering candy to a baby.

And goodness knows how many plays he eventually acted in during the four years he was at New Trier, but there had to be a lot. And also, at the same time, remember, he was acting in Bradley's other Shakespearean 16-mm movie epics. And so the years passed, until our senior high school year arrived, and then it became my turn to shine. And I did this by winning an oratorical contest. This was an extracurricular activity at New Trier in which contestants stood in front of a group of judges, mostly English language teachers, and recited from memory a twenty-minute speech written by a famous writer. In my case, it was one of Tolstoy's; *A Russian.* And I won!

And so there I was. A minor high school celebrity with my name headlined in the school paper and also being awarded a large silver cup with my name engraved on it (and which I carried around in the school's hallways to show it off before returning it). This, I thought, proved I was an actor; and so why not try out for a part in the school's senior play? And I did: and lo and behold I was offered the lead. The play was *Our Town,* and the lead was a Stage Manager who comes on stage at the beginning of act one and introduces the audience to the characters that each actor is portraying, and who after being introduced leaves the stage to begin the role. And me, I kept appearing from time to time to talk to the audience.

And so now the tryouts are over and the show's director, who was also the school's drama coach, and a very caring person, walks up to me, who had remained on the stage after the tryouts, and he asks, Can I talk to you? And I said sure, and so in a very nice way he wants to know if I wouldn't mind stepping aside and letting Charlton have the lead. He continues, saying the reason he's asking is that he believes Charlton, after working so hard during the past four years as the leading actor in all of the plays he had directed, deserved it. And I said okay (And why not? What did I know about acting?) So instead of playing the lead I took a minor role, and the play went on with Charlton in the lead role I had given up. And remember, this all happened when the two of us were seventeen years old.

DOOLITTLE

HESTON

Come 1945, marking the end of World War II, Charlton, having served in the Army Air Forces, and I in the Navy, returned to continue our schooling at Evanston, Illinois's Northwestern University in which both of us had enrolled in 1941: he went on to major in drama, and I in girls. During those first two years at N.U. we were members of the same fraternity and became friends, but after we returned from the war we saw little of each other.

And so, after graduating from N.U. Charlton, with his wife, Lydia, who also had attended N.U., after a long list of acting jobs in theater and TV caught the eye of Hollywood film producer Hal B. Wallis, who went on to help him get star billing in such epics as *The Ten Commandments*, *Ben Hur*, and my favorite, *Planet of the Apes*.

But what about the several 16-mm films that Charlton had acted in while we were both teenagers at New Trier? The answer, and it may be apocryphal, is that David Bradley took them with him when he went to Hollywood in the 1950's to seek work as a film editor and he used them as a way of helping him land a job. And it may have worked, because the last I know, David was employed in the 50s as a film editor at a major studio. As to where the 16-mm Charlton films that we produced may be right now? I have no idea.

And me? In the 1930's when New Trier's acting teacher asked me if it was okay by me to have Charlton take my place as the leading actor in *Our Town*, I should have told him to drop dead. Because who knows, thanks to a Hollywood actors' agent who just might have been sitting among New Trier's theater audience the day *Our Town* was featured, and turning to his wife sitting next to him, may have said: "Mabel, look at that kid Harry act! Someday he's going to be a big star!" And so, as time passed, it could have then been *me*, and not Charlton Heston who would have been chosen for the lead in *Planet of the Apes*. But that's the way the ball of life bounces.

*None of these plays were ever filmed as totally written by the Charlton-Bradley film team. Instead, they were produced as excerpts running no more than twenty-minutes each, with Charlton Heston always featured in the lead and accompanying him, a few of New Trier's aspiring teenage actors. Bradley was the cameraman who followed the actors around as he held onto his 16-mm camera with its black-and-white film.. Locations included places like the front of Chicago's Marshall Field Museum and inside the garden of Chicago's Art Institute, as well as in the backyard of Bradley's home and in his living room in Winnetka, Illinois.

Howdy Doody

Recollections #6:

It was six PM on a weekday in New York City in 1950 when millions of home TV sets all across the U.S. of A blinked on, revealing a group of a dozen or so boys and girls, ages five to fifteen, from many nationalities standing in a boxed area nicknamed *the Peanut Gallery* and gesturing wildly as an off-cameraman's voice shouts: "Hey kids, what time is it?" And the kids screamed back: "It's Howdy Doody time!" And thus began a continuing episode of the *Howdy Doody* TV show which ran on NBC's New York station and later on other stations from 1947 to 1960.

Howdy was a freckle-faced, red-haired wooden puppet, I guess you'd call it a marionette, manipulated by strings operated by an off-camera hand. And always standing on his stage he had a close companion, Captain Bob Smith, playing the role of Buffalo Bob, wearing a cowboy shirt who sat next to Howdy and the stage. The two would engage in conversations but were never seen together doing so. It went like this: when Bob was speaking to Howdy, the two were on camera, and when Howdy answered him, the camera cut to Howdy alone, and then when Bob spoke again, it cut back to show them both. This because Bob Smith was also Howdy's voice, and it wouldn't do for viewers to see Bob's lips moving at the same time as Howdy's.

And while Smith was an integral part of the show, most of the time he was off camera, letting Howdy be the star.*

And so what had I working that year as a TV commercial copywriter at the Grant Advertising Agency ad in Chicago, to do with the show? The commercials I was assigned to create were intended to sell Ovaltine, a high-energy chocolate drink for kids such as those who watched the *Howdy Doody* show, and for which the agency's time buyers had bought three minutes of the show's time to run one day a week. After being written by me, and approved by Ovaltine executives, copies of the commercials were faxed to the show's producers in New York where they became part of its telecast.

All to the good, except for one fly in the ointment. There was a crazy network rule, long since rescinded, which prohibited the name of the product or service it was selling to be mentioned until fifteen seconds of the commercial's sixty-or thirty-second had passed. Eureka! Now here was a chance for me not only to be a TV commercial writer but to also become a big time TV show writer, albeit a mere fifteen-second one. And how did I do this? I came up with visual concepts which were designed to last a lot longer than fifteen seconds, and thus it appeared as if what I had created was an integral part of the show. For example one was the Ovaltine Balloon Doodle. This was a visual gimmick used at the start of every *Howdy Doody*-Ovaltine sponsored fifteen-minute segment. And it consisted of a six-foot-long, two-foot-tall board standing on a table in front of the camera, and printed on it were the letters O-V-A-L-T-I-N-E. And in front of each letter, and concealing it, was a floating balloon attached to the table by its string.

And standing next to it was Clarabell the Clown holding a long nail. So that when the announcer shouts, "Hey kids, what time is it?," the kids would yell back, "It's O-V-A-L-T-I-N-E time." Yelling out each letter separately so that Clarabell, using the nail, and in sync with each letter being yelled, would pop each of the balloons and thus uncover the entire Ovaltine name.

But this wasn't all. The word *Ovaltine* is made up of eight letters, the same number as in an eight-note musical scale. And so what could be more appropriate than to have the station's organist, who along with each of the kids in the Peanut Gallery yelling out the letters, to also play eight musical chords in ascending order as each balloon was being popped. And that's what Clarabell did. And all of this is what I had originated for it to be used at the beginning of every one of the *Hoody Doody*-Ovaltine sponsored episodes. ("Look, Ma Harry's in show biz!")

And here's another example (and I promise not to bore you with more, although there are lots). It went like this: I'd have Rex Marshall, the show's announcer, speak on-camera just before one of my sixty second Ovaltine commercials was to be aired on one of the *Hoody Doody* episodes.

The words he spoke were written by me and Rex spoke them as he stood in front of the camera all by himself, as follows:

"Hey kids, it's too bad Howdy Doody is on vacation. Because I bet if he wasn't in [he speaks a made-up place] he could solve this mysterious message which just came to me over the Lollapalooza before the show began [if convenient, have the message actually come over the Lollapalooza, if not, write the message on a piece of paper and have Rex hold it up]. And then after several minutes had passed, with Rex continuing to speak, he finally gets around to mentioning the sponsor's name, which is Ovaltine, and that's when the Ovaltine commercial actually begins.

But why was this happening? That is, why spend so many minutes of the valuable show time telecasting a bunch of trivial nonsense before getting around to mentioning the name of its sponsor? Instead, why not telecast only the commercial itself without having to pad it with a lot of extraneous talking which would use up some of the show's time? Well, I'll tell you.

It was because Eddie Kean, the *Hoody Doody* show's chief writer was to use a show-biz term "vamping." Why was he doing this? Because his job was to originate some twenty or more different sponsored Hoody Doody shows every week; each fifteen-minutes in length, and each original. And that meant not only did he have to come up with a different plot for each fifteen- minute segment but it also had to get a high rating or else the show's sponsors would become very unhappy.

As a result, Eddie was going bananas. He needed assistance, and one way to do so was to call me. My phone would ring, and he'd say. "Hi, it's Eddie. Can you give me a hand? Could you maybe pad your ad copy, or better yet, give it a longer intro?" Anything which would allow the commercial to take up more of the show's time. And since the rule was that we weren't allowed to mention the sponsoring product's name in a commercial until after the first fifteen seconds of it had begun, the alternative was to do just as I have described above: to "vamp and to pad." And vamping and padding is what I did best.

But now as an aside, here is a sample of the sort of the additional "paddings" I would include in my commercials, which not only made my commercials more fun to watch, but also did what Eddie Kean had asked me to do; namely to help him contribute to the writing of the *Howdy Doody* shows. What follows is an example, and has to do with the Ovaltine balloon doodle. Instructions of this sort were always written in bold letters.

Camera focuses on CB (Clarabell the Clown) standing next to the balloon doodle and in CB's hand there is a long steel nail. And of the original eight balloons only one balloon is left inflated because the seven others have already been popped by CB. And so now using the nail CB jabs and jabs at this single balloon and in sync with each jab the organ plays a loud note. But all to no avail because the balloon does not pop. Finally, CB in frustration stamps his foot and the balloon pops and deflates. This is accompanied by a long and loud crescendo of organ music. CB jumps up and down with joy as BS (Bob Smith) and HD Howdy Doody move into the picture and BS claps CB on the back.

And so it went for another half year until after I left Grant Advertising, Inc., and Chicago, and moved to New York City. There, I landed a job as one of four Creative Directors at the Ted Bates Co., a New York City ad agency and stayed with it for sixteen years.

*Three of the show's many other characters (and some of my favorites) were Flub-A-Dub, who was eight animals in one; a duck's head, a cocker spaniel's ears, a giraffe's neck, a pig's tail, a cat's whiskers, and body parts of three other animals including an elephant. And then there was Dilly Dally with a big D on his sweater who could wiggle his ears. My favorite of them all, PrincessSummerFallWinterSpring, introduced first as a puppet and later transformed into a beautiful young girl.

Tough Times

Recollections #7:

In 1933 I was ten years old when my fifty-five-year old father, Henry Pelouze (what a name!) Doolittle died He left behind a widowed wife, two pre-teenage sons and a yet-to-be paid $8,000 mortgage on our house in Winnetka, Illinois, a northern Chicago suburb on the Lake Michigan shore.

As a Chicago-based patent attorney employed by the International Harvester Company (it made small farm tractors and big trucks), he had a salary of $26,000 a year (these days equivalent to $500,000). But much of that money went to support his sixtyish-year-old widowed mother and her four thirtyish-year-old spinster daughters, [his sisters] living in a minor mansion, staffed with two servants, a chauffeur, and cook in Washington, DC. The rest of his income went to provide for us: his wife, my mother, and his two sons, plus the upkeep of our Winnetka home, along with the maintenance of a six-cylinder, four-door 1932 Chevrolet.

1933 marked the height, or should I say depth, of the thirties' depression, which lasted until the start of World War II. That year, 1933, a loaf of bread at the local Penny-Wenny's cost ten cents, as did a gallon of gasoline at the nearby Standard Oil gas station (eight cents on certain Saturdays). Almost no one ever bought more than five gallons at a time, paying for it with a fifty- cent coin, carried for just that purpose and no longer in circulation. Seeing a major feature movie cost ten cents for kids under twelve, and twenty-five cents for those twelve and older, as well as for adults.

Following my father's death, and after two months of waiting for a bid on our up-for-sale home, my mother said to heck with it, and we moved out. We took our beds, some furniture, dishes, and other things, and moved into a sixth-floor, two-bedroom apartment in the Winnetka village. As for rest of the stuff, it went to be held and sold at the local Episcopal Church's once-a-year rummage sale.

Now in the basement of the apartment house in which we lived was a small department store. And among other items, it featured children's, men's, and women's clothes. Looking for a way to make money, I approached its manager, and he gave me a job. My pay was fifty cents a day. And the job

meant arriving at the store after school and making sure that all the garments on its tables were neatly piled and attractively displayed at all

times. Reason for this was that many women, coming to the store to buy, let's say, shirts for their husbands had a habit of picking one up, unfolding it, and holding it out in front of them in order to examine it more closely. Then, if not liking it, tossing it back onto the table, leaving it crumpled up. And often, because the wife couldn't make up her mind as to which one to choose, the piles would grow six shirts deep. Thus, it was my job to "un-crumple" them and lay each back onto its table.

And this I was doing one afternoon when a lady shirt buyer, spotting me, came up to me and said: "Young man, can you help tell me which shirt size I should buy for my husband? He's six feet, and weighs two hundred pounds." And I? What did I, an eleven-year-old kid, know? So I shrugged and stepped away, leaving the poor soul looking bewildered.

And why was this? Because she thought I was one of the store's salespersons. That's right! Remember, this was 1933, and to see young kids doing adult jobs like I doing was commonplace.

Take the Illinois farms just west of Chicago, for example: on them were boys ten and under driving tractors and girls the same ages in kitchens helping their moms getting dinner ready to feed the entire family as well as the farm's hired hands.

And so I had an epiphany, an awakening. Why not really learn about men's shirts so the next time a wife asked me which one to buy, I would be able to discuss it in a sophisticated salesman's like manner. And that's what I did.

Then, when a wife asked that question I was able to answer: "Well, we offer a variety of colors; white, blue, pink, yellow, and a variety of fabrics and sizes; cotton, wool, nylon, ranging from a fourteen to seventeen-inch neck size and a sleeve length of twenty-eight to thirty-six inches." And next I'd ask: "How tall is your husband, and what does he weigh?" And let's say she said "Six feet and two hundred pounds," Then I'd reply "I suggest a white, nylon, sixteen-inch collar, and a thirty-six-inch sleeve." And she'd take it.

Well now, believe it or not, at age eleven, I became one of the store's top shirt salespersons, due to ladies arriving to buy shirts and telling the manager: "I want that kid in the men's shirt department because I've been told he really knows his shirts." It could only have happened in the 1930s.

Workplace Amenity?

Recollection #8:

One of the definitions of *Amenity*, as stated in *Google*, is, *"the pleasantness and attractiveness of a place."* And, when combined with the word *workplace*, best describes what sort of place at which you are employed should be. But unfortunately such a benign expression did not suit the place I ended up getting hired at a year after leaving the U.S. Navy in 1946.

This was a factory, owned by the International Harvester Co., and located in Chicago, Illinois' far Southwest Side. The product it produced was the FarMall Tractor, a small tractor suitable for use on small farms and able to be handled by small children. And now how in the world did I end up in such a position? Well, previously in 1946 I had applied to begin my first year at Northwestern University's Law School but was told I would have to wait months before I could start. And so what the heck, while waiting, why not also go to work?

And I accomplished this by calling on a former friend of my deceased father at the Harvester company's office asking him for a job. He says, "Hey kid, how'd you like to be the company president some day?" And I say, "Sure." So he says, "But you'll first have to start at the bottom. And so that's why I'm sending you to see [states a name] at our Farmall factory, and he's going to give you a job." And sure enough he did. But before I tell you about what kind of a job I it was you've got to hear about how I started out: this meant arriving at the factory gates at 7 AM to begin a weekly-seven hours-a-day shift.

I lived in Evanston and the Harvester factory was located at the corner of Chicago's Western Avenue and South 42nd street, resulting in taking me about an hour to drive to it in my secondhand 1936 Ford convertible. As an aside, Chicago's Western Avenue, whose north end begins at the borderline of Evanston and Chicago and then ran due south for more than 25 miles straight down to the Indiana state borderline, resulting in it being anointed with the accolade, "The Longest Straight City Road in the World," a term Chicagoans at that time were immensely proud of, and which they would brag about to every outsider they'd meet. ("We have the longest city straight road in the world. Whadda-you got?"). Yuck!

And so I arrived at the factory for my first day of work. This involved pushing a wheel barrel loaded with 100 pounds of wet sand up a narrow twelve inch board suspended twenty feet above the concrete floor and then dumping all its contents onto the cement floor in front of a worker with a shovel who would scoop it up and put it inside a mold which, after being fired up inside a 1,000 degree Centigrade furnace would produce a red hot steel ingot which would then be drop-forged, pressed into whatever shape needed. (Whew!)

But I didn't stay in that job for long. I soon found myself standing next to an enormous forty-foot-tall apparatus used for drop-forging. Which, according to *Google* is "A process used to shape metal into complex shapes by dropping a heavy hammer with a die on its face onto the work piece". And thank goodness I didn't have to operate it (two of their experienced factory workers did), I did have to stand next to it where my task was to pick up the newly shaped red-hot metal pieces that it produced. I did this by using a pair of three-foot-long tweezers held in my canvas gloved hands, followed by my using them to place the red hot pieces into a cutter, which in turn would trim off any of its excess metal.

Adding to this process was that each time the hammer hit the metal the collision produced an enormous bang. And this was made especially annoying when its operator, using his foot pedal, which caused the hammer to rise and fall, was pressed by him a dozen times per each piece being forged, and thus producing a dozen bangs! As for the entire process, meeting the *amenity* criterion, mentioned at the beginning of this story, was the drop-forge area a "pleasant and attractive place" in which to work? It didn't even come close. But I loved it.

Moreover, I soon found a way to compensate for the bangs and the 100- degree area in which I found myself. I stuffed my ears with cotton and had service bring in an enormous electric fan, its blades the size of a small airplane's propeller, and had it placed fifteen feet behind me where it blew cool air on me, and soon everything was hunky-dory.

And now, one last incident: There I was at work one morning on the factory assembly line a week or two before I was scheduled to go on to N.U.'s law school, when three men in jeans and work shirts showed up, the shortest and oldest standing in the middle cradling an official looking clipboard in his arms, and he says: Kid, can I talk to you?" And I, laying aside my work tools, go up to him and say, "Sure." And he says he thinks it would be great idea for me to join his union. Except that wasn't quite the way it was put.

Instead, he was assisted by two six-feet-tall, 200-plus-pound cohorts, one standing on his left side with his arms folded across his chest, and the other standing on his right side and on whose hands were a pair of thick rubberized canvas gloves, with the right glove holding a foot-long steel monkey wrench.

And what followed went like this: "Y' know, kid, I think it would be a good (slap) idea if you (slap) were to (slap, slap) join our union!" The slap sounds were created by the gloved guy, who while holding the monkey wrench in his right hand, pounded it into the palm of his canvas-covered left hand. The implication being that if I didn't agree with such a delightful invitation that little ol' monkey wrench night find a new target, like my head.

Well, needless to say, it was one which didn't appeal to me, or should I say, the way it was put to me did not.

Now, remember all this took place some 67 years ago, when the events of World War II were still in everyone's memory, and the goal of a 1940s national full employment had yet to be achieved, and union officials like the three goons with the monkey wrench would never be union tolerated today. As for me, it was a great learning experience.

As for my accepting their (generous?) invitation which I have detailed above, and which was put to me put to in such an original manner, I answered nothing, and instead turned and quietly walked away.

Kukla, Fran & Ollie

Recollection #9:

Let's see. The war had ended and I'd been discharged (honorably, my discharge papers read, whatever that was supposed to imply). And then in the mid 1940's I went to Northwestern University Law School in Chicago. And after six months, when that didn't pan out (my law professor said I had too much imagination to be a lawyer), I sat down and said to myself: "Hey, you've got to get your life in order and find something really fun and useful to do." And I did. It was in television.

At that time, TV broadcasting and its viewing, was in its infancy (my home TV screen, for instance, measured just two feet by one foot, with all its images in black and white). There were just two stations in New York City, NBC and CBS, and just one on the West Coast, LA's CBS; and only one in Chicago, WBKB, owned by the California Paramount Studio chain.

And so how was I going to get into the TV station business? I solved that problem by contacting a former N.U. fraternity brother who had a big job at a Chicago NBC radio station, and his advice was to be able to prove to a TV station manager that I had a theater background. And then how to do that? Easy, it turned out. My frat brother told me go up to Highland Park, a suburb north of Chicago, and try to get a job with a summer stock theater which was to open in July (summer stock meaning it functioned in summer only and also employed actors and staff for that time only).

Its name was *the Tent House Theater*, a huge at one-time canvas circus tent, with a gravel floor and 1,200 wooden seats all surrounding a circular five-foot-tall wooden stage. In short, it was a prime example of "theater in the round," a theatrical rage at that time. For the actors, entrances on and exits off were facilitated by a set of steps leading up from the ground to the stage floor, plus a bridge attached at its back enabling the actors who stood behind a large black curtain to step aboard the stage whenever cued.

And so in June, after driving up to Highland Park from my Evanston home, I arrived at the theater, its tent now in the process of being raised in a vacant lot five miles west of town. And I, going up to the theater's manager, a major investor in the show, and from Seattle, asked for a job: ticket taker, rug sweeper, anything, no matter how trivial, in order for me to be able to say that I had had show-business experience. And he said, "How'd you like to be the stage manager?" and I said, "Sure," and he then added, "But there's no money," and I said, "That's okay." And so that's how I began my theatrical career, which later led to my getting hired by WBKB, at that time Chicago's only TV station.

Highland Park's Tent House Theater turned out to be a gold mine for its owners and a Mount Everest-sized educational theater experience for me. During the next three months and six-day-a week, and twelve-hour days, I learned to help doing just about everything: set building, lighting, furniture choosing, costuming, and most important, casting. All in all we produced eight plays, including one of George Bernard Shaw's, and one of Tennessee William's. Best of all was getting to know actors and how different they seemed to be from "ordinary" people, dedicated as they were to narcissism and obsessed with achieving renown. And I loved them all.

The summer season ended and the Tent House Theater contingent, including all of its actors, shoved off to Seattle.

And me? Now that I had a theater background, I dropped by WBKB's office and was hired on the spot: they needed a "dolly pusher," someone who stands behind the cameraman and helps him move his wheel-attached camera from place to place.

This was in 1947, the beginning of WBKB's telecast of *Kukla, Fran & Ollie,* and soon it was my good fortune to become its "boom man." This meant standing in front of stage holding an extended steel pole with a microphone at is end and manipulating its height and closeness for the purpose of picking up Burr's and Fran's conversations. All this took place in a small bare room with seats for no more than twelve guests, each an adult, especially chosen from among tens of thousands of its fans who had written asking for tickets.

But it wasn't long before certain TV biggies decided the show would get higher ratings of telecasted by the NBC network, which meant it leaving Chicago's WBKB and moving it to New York. And while no tears were shed, the move resulted in Burr Tillstrom, *Kukla, Fran & Ollie's* creator, throwing a farewell for those of us who had worked his show. And it went like this:

Burr had had two of WBKB's crew move the entire *Kukla, Fran & Ollie* stage to a spot within WBKB's largest studio, and there they set it up as if to be camera ready. He then invited the two stagehands, Fran Allison, Bulla Zachary (his producer), and me to come in and sit down. All of its doors were locked and it became a "closed set," which meant absolutely no one else was allowed inside. Burr entered, nodded, and went behind *KFO's* stage, which lighted up, and hello! There they were, Ollie nodding and grinning, and Kukla waving at us.

From then on it was Burr's show, with his two marionettes, Kukla and Ollie, assisting him. For about half an hour, he reminisced, relating the history of how the show had originated, along with some of its highlights: this included slight digs at me and Fran, telling how I, on the rarest of occurrences, would lower the boom, which allowed the mike to be seen (an absolute no-no): and how Fran would stand (but rarely) in front of Ollie so that he had to peek around her, which drove him crazy, evidenced by Ollie shaking his head and banging his long white tooth on the stage, all this making Fran and me laugh.

And now, with Burr's creations' goodbyes over, and with each now lying seemingly asleep at the stage's edge, Burr appeared standing in their places. In one of his hands he held a bottle of Johnnie Walker Red Label scotch and in the other, a glass. And after pouring a couple of ounces, he raised the glass, toasted us, and thanked us for all of our help. Then, after putting the glass down and still holding the bottle, he waved, turned, and walked away, and I never saw him again. Several months later I left WBKB to begin a wonderful new adventure.

Note: *Kukla, Fran & Ollie* photos and those of Burr and Fran as well as the stage can be seen on Google, and I assume copies can be obtained by ordering them through Google's printed instructions.

A Happy Landing

Recollections #10:

The year was 1980, and I and my South Korean bride, twenty-four-year old Misook, were living in a lovely apartment in Rosebank, one of Johannesburg South Africa's most elite and beautiful suburbs. Misook, born and raised in South Korea, had flown to join me from America where she had just graduated from the University of Southern Indiana, located in Evansville, Indiana, and where I had worked for the past three years as a creative director at a local Evansville advertising agency, and also where I had met and fallen in love with her. And I was now going to be hired to do similar work at an ad agency head quartered at Rosebank. It in turn, was an overseas subsidiary of New York City's Ted Bates ad agency, and which owned almost all of the Johannesburg company.

At that time, since it was against South African law for two individuals of different races, and colors, to get married (according to it, I was "white" and Misook "colored"), we flew north to Zimbabwe, where the ceremony was performed. Thus, having married me she became an American citizen, and there was nothing the crusty old S.A. government lawyers could do about trying to toss her out of their country. Fortunately, such a ridiculous law no longer exists in South Africa.

And so, life and work went sailing along with both me and Misook working at the Bates ad agency, and I occasionally playing golf at the Rosebank country club, and both of us making new friends. Two of which, Jonathan Barr from London, and his wife, Helga from Sweden and a U.S. citizen, became our closest. He worked with me as an account executive at the Bates agency, and she did her own thing, staying in their lovely Rosebank home alone and creating new recipes which she tried out on us.

Then one day Jonathan says to me, "Let's go to on safari at Londolozi."

Its full name was the Londolozi Game Preserve, and it encompassed 35,000 acres situated in the heart of the Sabi Sand Game Preserve within the border of South Africa's Kruger National Park and far west of Johannesburg. The plan was for us to stay at one of the park's five private lodges, and then be taken in an open jeep driven by a local guide to look for

and hopefully, to get close to some of Africa's wild animals. The lodge at which we chose to stay was at Verty Camp. And not only did we did get close to a bunch of South Africa's wildlife, we were also privileged to get to see, THE BIG FIVE. This was a title used to describe the five animals every Kruger Park visitor not only *wanted to, but had to, was dying to,* to see from among the dozens of other kinds that roamed its jungles. The five were: the elephant, the lion, the giraffe, the gorilla, and the cheetah. And did we get to see all five? You bet! And to prove it Misook and I were each rewarded a badge to pin on our shirts. It read: "I SAW THE BIG FIVE!"

Now how did I and Misook get to Londolozi? We flew there via private plane, a single engine 150HP Cessna with fixed landing gear. And Jonathan, who had a pilot's license, sat at the plane's controls, and I, who sat next to him, served as "navigator" with my eyes focused on the front panel's gages, calling out compass headings and distances traveled. Our two wives sat behind us in a small space perched on a hard leather seat. Driving to Londolozi from JoBurg would have taken five hours, but by flying we got there in two and a half.

After about an hour out contact by radio with the JoBurg airport ceased and so navigation-wise we were on our own. We were limited by law to fly no higher than 6,000 feet, and since many of the country's mountains were at that height, we had to dodge around a few, and that was a bit hairy. But we made it, and we landed at a small Londolozi private air strip, parking the Cessna next to the only other plane there. But before taking a cab to go our hotel, I told the airport's lone mechanic to make sure our plane's gasoline tanks were full before we came back for our return flight. And he did, after I had handed him a fistful of S.A. Rands.

From there we went on to the Verty Camp, staying there for four days and doing stuff such as I've described above. That over, we took a cab back to the airfield preparing to board the Cessna for our return trip hone. And just for the heck of it, Jonathan had the lone airport guy take a long wooden measuring gauge and stick it inside of one of the plane's gas tanks to determine how much fuel was actually there. Well, whaddaya know, it was empty, zero, gone, as it also was in the other plane's tank. So I and Jonathan left the airstrip to report this to the local police, located a few miles away, and their reply was, "Duh, we don't know nuttin," and it was obvious they were the ones who had siphoned out the gasoline and were making money for themselves by selling it on the black market.

So wat to do next? Our inquiry revealed that the nearest source for getting more gasoline was in a town a half hour's drive away. And this led to us taking a cab to Hertz, renting one of its cars, and picking up a 100-gallon empty steel drum from Hertz and putting it inside our car's trunk. And then we drove to the nearest gas station. There we had the drum filled to the brim with 110-octane high gasoline and put back into the car's trunk, but with its lid left open. Driving back to our tiny airfield, Jonathan, who must have thought he was still aboard the Cessna, drove at 90 miles an hour, with the gasoline-filled drum bouncing up and down inside the trunk. It gave me the willies, but we made it to the airfield safely.

Now, the problem was how were we to get the gasoline out of its container and into the Cessna's two fuel tanks? Well, thanks to help from the airfield's lone mechanic and a buddy who showed up to assist, it was accomplished as follows. Holding a six foot-long rubber tube, the mechanic placed one end through a hole punched out of the drum's lid, it going down into the gasoline, and this followed by his placing the other end of the tube into his mouth and sucking on it. A few drops got into his mouth, which he spitted out, but the rest flowed from the drum up inside of the tube, and out of its other end and into the fuel tank. This procedure was repeated with the other tank, leaving both tanks filled. Or were they? Seems 100-gallons wasn't enough: the tanks were short by five gallons, which didn't seem to matter at the time, but turned out to be crucial later.

On we went, taking off from the little airfield, and waving goodbye to Londolozi, while heading east for JoBurg two and half hours away. But the flight wasn't continuous. Halfway there, Helga announced she had to use the "lieu" (bathroom), and since there wasn't one on board, Jonathan looking out the plane's window for a landing field luckily spotted what could be a place for one, a small dirt runway used by the area's flying farmers. So we landed, with Helga going into one of its shacks to use the bathroom, and then returning to the plane. Minutes later, and with Jonathan gunning the engine at full throttle we took off, and this meant that the plane's engine was gulping a large amount of fuel during its ascent as compared to what would be normally used at level flight. A factor which had a lot to do with what happened later

Time passed, and soon we were spotting some of the city's buildings and, beyond them, the giant Johannesburg airport itself, about six miles off in the distance. Our plane was at an altitude of 5,000 feet, and we were doing about 110 mph, when suddenly its engine began to bang and sputter (bang, bang. sputter, sputter). This was a clear-cut signal that it was starved for fuel. And all of this made me feel a bit uneasy, to say the least.

So here we were, five miles away from touching down and aboard a plane whose engine was having hiccups. But these didn't last long, because as we got closer to the airport, now a few miles away, the engine quit, and instead of being a plane, it had turned into a propeller-less glider and, having done so, needed to be handled as if it was one.

Me? I wasn't panicky, but I was nervous. But not Jonathan. Acting and looking cool as a cucumber, he gets on the horn (the plane's radio) and, calling JoBurg's airport control tower, gives it the plane's wing numbers and saying, "Mayday, Mayday, Mayday [a universally acknowledged term used by pilots whenever confronted by a bad situation], this is [he identifies himself]," and a calm voice answers from the control, "Hello [our plane's ID #], what's the trouble?" And Jonathan, replying, gives him the whole bit: our height and speed, and from where we were coming, who's on board, and concluding by telling the control tower:

"Our engine's dead, but we're high enough and I think I can glide us in."

[In aviation parlance, he was going to make a "dead stick landing"].

And so, at 5,000 feet, three miles from the landing strip, we start our glide, skimming over tall city buildings, crowded highways, and a few turned up faces staring at us, and finally, ever so gently, we can feel all three of the Cessna's wheels touching down on the runway. And whaddaya know? It continues to roll, on and on, finally coming to a complete stop right in front of a fire engine and ambulance which the airport's tower had ordered to stand by, just in case. But I'm not sure, after climbing out of our Cessna, if I got down on my knees and kissed the ground, but I like to think I did.

That was the end of our adventure; to be followed by our two friends leaving Ted Bates, South Africa and retuning to London and their home, and Misook and I doing the same, only going in another direction, to the good old U.S. of A.

Printed in the United States
By Bookmasters